TEXTS FOR NOTHING

TEXTS FOR NOTHING

TEXTES POUR RIEN
AFTER S.B.

HAROLD MENDEZ

TABLE OF CONTENTS

PREFACE
TRICIA VAN ECK

THE MOMENT BEFORE WRITING IS THE BLANK PAGE. THE MOMENT BEFORE PAINTING IS THE BLANK CANVAS. THE MOMENT BEFORE MUSIC IS THE SILENCE.

This extended yet static moment is the setting of Harold Mendez's *Texts for Nothing / Textes pour rien*. The title, as Mendez writes in his Introduction, refers to the silent measure before a performance, the breath before a song, the stasis before an action. While references to Samuel Beckett's *Waiting for Godot* abound, there is no waiting for someone or something to arrive. Instead, in this suspended and measured moment, which Mendez refers to as "a soundless interval conveying nothing but setting the tempo and so an essential part of the musical whole," his characters—BRAILLE TEETH and NOBODY—confront the metaphysical desire for meaning. In this measuring of absence and of substance we encounter the dilemma of the story—the story of the self—and the struggle of rendering into language how one recognizes, defines, and constitutes oneself and the world.

Mendez explains his text as a conversation between two characters in an "abstract and universal" landscape. It begins with a fence, a border, or what is described as an "enfilade of pensioners" a connected formation of gnarled mesquite posts, each opening onto the next. Mesquite wood establishes the setting as an arid or semi-arid desert area. A symbol of tenacious temperament, mesquite can withstand drought or "the crisis" which remains unnamed in the text.

Drawing from this text in 2008, Mendez applied packing tape on a gallery wall alluding to the optical changes of an inaccessible location in the desert and the metaphor of a fence.[1] About this installation he wrote: "Deserts, real and metaphorical, have historically captured the human imagination as thresholds of transcendence and becoming, but also as sites of penance, death, and undoing."[2]

Within this desolate landscape, Mendez's characters punctuate the empty silence by emitting collaged words and ideas. Rather than creating much of the language which BRAILLE TEETH and NOBODY speak, Mendez arranges appropriated language (with endnotes) into a kaleidoscope of verbal associations and impressions. Mendez's polyphonic montage of diverse sources—existentialist plays, Vietnam War novels, foreign and American novels, films, and television programs—all share an essential atmosphere and mood, a kind of grainy palette which echoes the impalpable line between that of immateriality and materiality and being and becoming. In the characters' quest for subjectivity and self-knowledge Mendez's appropriated text substantiates their existential dilemma since embedded within the speech act, is a necessary choice of words and bodily delivery.

NOBODY confronts the empty silence of nothingness by looking down and saying: "Look at this stuff. No growth, no decay, no streaming fluids" to which BRAILLE TEETH replies, "a sort of perverse signature." NOBODY counters by looking at the expanse around them responding, "... but I am very fond of such scenery. The distance in it is fluid and the contours vague, and thus perhaps it resembles my own position."

---

1   In November 2008 Mendez created a site specific installation for the *12 x 12: UBS New Art/New Work* series at the Museum of Contemporary Art, Chicago
2   Mendez quoted from Rocio Magaña. "Bodies on the Line: Life, Death, and Authority on the Arizona-Mexico Border." (Unpublished doctoral dissertation) University of Chicago

Displaced from the world of referential meaning, NOBODY and BRAILLE TEETH are thrust into an ontological inner universe where each attempts to construct meaning. Perhaps then, Mendez's text is a meditation on the indeterminate self with its constituent parts of consciousness, ego, rational self, emotional self, soul, and physical body, all in conflict over which will "represent." Throwing open Descartes' body mind dualism, it's as if the mouth—BRAILLE TEETH—strives to connect not with its mind but its consciousness—NOBODY. Within this merciless negotiation between the self as subject, as knower and the self as object, witness, and protagonist[3] lies the difficult process of integration, of becoming, of uncovering the "truth" of one's self, and conveying this to a world that seems dead.

In this abyss, lies the inner turmoil of suspended potentiality. Searching between sensory impressions of what is and thoughts of what might be, the characters face Kierkergaard's "fear and trembling," the suffering of choice, of creation, of existence, where one begins to confront one's deepest fears and anxieties.[4] This is illustrated in the text:

> BRAILLE TEETH. It's the start that's difficult.
> NOBODY. You can start from anything.
> BRAILLE TEETH. Yes, but you have to decide.

IN THE BEGINNING THE WORD WAS MADE FLESH?

If the mouth is the liminal intersection between both the material, corporeal world and the realm of language and ideas, then what is the material presence of the self? Could NOBODY represent the conscious self, through a kind of an "immaterial sensibility": a way of seeing, perceiving, and living in the world?[5] In Antonin Artaud's conclusion of his radio play *To Have Done with the Judgement of God* (*Pour en Finir*

---

3 Antonio Damasio, *Self Comes to Mind: Constructing the Conscious Brain* (New York: Pantheon Books, 2010) p. 9–12.

4 While Søren Kierkegaard's 1843 treatise on the Biblical story of Abraham's sacrifice of his son Isaac, "Fear and Trembling," examines Abraham's difficult act of extreme choice between society, self, and the infinite, Kierkegaard emphasizes that this existential angst is embedded in all encounters that require choice.

5 Philippe Vergne and Julie Caniglia, *Yves Klein and the patron saint of lost causes*. Interview with Julie Caniglia ; 27 Jan. 2011 [cited 2011 January 26] Available from: http://blogs.walkerart.org/visualarts/2011/01/27/yves-klein-and-the-patron-saint-of-lost-causes/

avec le Jugement de Dieu), he discusses the power of this position: "When you will have made him a body without organs, then you will have delivered him from all his automatic reactions and restored him to his true freedom."[6] Removed from the material world and devoid of a final shape, Mendez's characters with liminal names—a mouth that suggests sign language and a body that has no form—represent a kind of freedom from conforming and a movement toward a singular becoming, like Kierkegaard, who before embarking on a career of writing, wrote:

> *What I really need is to get clear about what I must do, not what I must know, except in so far as a certain knowledge must precede every action ... the crucial thing is to find a truth which is true for me, to find the idea for which I am willing to live and die...*[7]

> *I certainly do not deny that I still recognize an imperative of understanding and that through it one can work upon men, but it must be taken up into my life, and that is what I now recognize as the most important thing.*[8]

THE IMMATERIAL OBJECT

"To all appearances, the artist acts like a mediumistic being who, from the labyrinth beyond time and space seeks his way out to a clearing."[9]

Moving out of the labyrinth—of why attempt, what to do, where to begin, and how to start—into the solidity of form and materialism, a metaphysical fear of shaping and producing meaning and form can easily occur. This is reflected in Gustave Flaubert's definition of materialism in *The Dictionary of Accepted Ideas:* "Materialism: Utter the

---

6   Susan Sontag, ed. *Antonin Artaud, Selected Writings* (Berkeley: University of California Press, 1973) p. 571. Also available from: http://ndirty.cute.fi/~karttu/tekstit/artaud.htm

7   Søren Kierkegaard, Howard Vincent Hong, Edna H. Hong, *Søren Kierkegaard's Journals and Papers, Part 1* (Bloomington: Indiana University Press, 1976) p. 34.

8   The Journals of Søren Kierkegaard, A Selection Edited and Translated by Alexandeer Dru (Oxford: Oxford University Press, 1938) p. 15.

9   Robert Lebel, ed. *Marcel Duchamp* (New York: Grove Press, 1959) p. 77–8. Also available from: http://www.wisdomportal.com/Cinema-Machine/Duchamp-CreativeAct.html

word with horror, stressing each syllable."[10] By creating a fully defined material form, the pathway leading to further choices regarding meaning and content is thrown open as Barbara Rose pointed out in her review of early Minimalist works: "... the blankness, the emptiness and vacuum of content is as easily construed as an occasion for spiritual contemplation as it is a nihilistic denial of the world."[11] Fearing the responsibility of creating a definitive form or content, at the end of Act I Mendez's characters resist the world of representation:

> BRAILLE TEETH. (*Deeply serious. His voice rising to match* NOBODY'S.) But we are each that, while we live, however much we resist: almost without surface, barely contained...
> BRAILLE TEETH. (*In pensive thought.*) What and how much had I lost by trying to do only what was expected of me instead of what I myself had wished to do?
> NOBODY. (*After a sympathetic pause. With a private knowledge.*) He imagined the pain of the world to be like some formless parasitic being seeking out the warmth of human souls wherein to incubate and he thought he knew what made one liable to its visitations. What he had not known was that it was mindless and so had no way to know the limits of those souls and what he feared was that there might be no limits.

If as a society, we increasingly interact with representations of things rather than the things themselves, then perhaps our attention needs to focus less on the form of the representation itself, but what the representation reveals. If Mendez's text is a story of a narrative of the self, in Act II NOBODY endeavors to confront the world of form and becoming in an attempt to find meaning. Nobody hears the voices of those who "talk about their lives." BRAILLE TEETH says: "To have lived is not enough for them ... To be dead is not enough for them." Since one's life is often measured and explained through personal narrative—the self creating a unique story—NOBODY wishes, like the voices he hears, to be defined by their story:

---

10   Robert Smithson, "A Museum of Language in the Vicinity of Art," Art International, March 1968, p. 21.
11   Barbara Rose, "ABC Art," "Art in America," vol. 53 (October–November 1965) p. 69.

BRAILLE TEETH. (*More or less to himself.*) He
would like it to be my fault that he has no story, of
course he has no story, that's no reason for trying
to foist one on me. That's how he reasons, wide of
the mark, but wide of what mark, answer us that.

NOBODY. There has to be one, it seems, once
there is speech, no need of a story, a story is not
compulsory, just a life, that's the mistake I made,
one of the mistakes, to have wanted a story for
myself, whereas life alone is enough.

Ultimately NOBODY realizes his mistake in wanting some meaning
or material form beyond his authentic existence. Similarly, Hamish
Fulton, an artist whose art is walking, makes work which he calls
No(thing). Fulton leaves no form, mark, or intervention on the land
through which he walks. Rather than produce something material, his
work shifts the focus from the object to the experience of his walks.
The experience has a life of its own and does not need to be made
into art. As Fulton has written: "My idea is to support the creativity of
artists; what the art looks like is of less importance."[12] Following from
this statement, perhaps Mendez's text is not meant to be material, but
a mode of future creation.

If the progress of the future is based on a recollection of the past,
which in turn gives meaning to the present, then without life stories
there is no apparent future for Mendez's characters in the text. For
Mendez, however, the text is future, present, and past. It is a reposi-
tory of Mendez's ideas and images, language and matter, where, as
if a touchstone, he goes when beginning his art. Like Taoism's
famous doctrine of *wu-wei*, which can be translated as "non-action"
or knowing when to act and when not to act, for Mendez the text is
like a battery, a holding pen of the tension and conflict of becoming.
Texts for Nothing / Textes pour rien—the space or non-space of existential angst—is where Mendez aligns himself in its creative quietude
and powerful stasis of becoming.

---

12   Hamish Fulton, "Life in Film: Hamish Fulton" *Frieze Magazine:* Issue 108, Jun.–Aug.
      2007. Available from: http://www.frieze.com/issue/article/life_in_film_hamish_fulton/

INTRODUCTION

A note on the text and title:

What follows is a text that reorganizes, as narrative, a fictional conversation between two characters who share "a difficult journey, across a landscape abstract and universal yet sharply particularized ... Yet the place, like the body, is 'unimportant,' and descriptions annihilate themselves: 'Glorious prospect, but for the mist.' An exact sense of place is paradoxically the nowhere of a story that moves away from external 'description' toward a narrative about narrating."[i] The ensuing sections of dialogue, line by line, are appropriated from literary sources, music, film, television, and personal writings that function as a framework; while dealing with subjects, which address conventions of place and humanity where something seemed to occur. These issues are grounded in an existentialist stratum that circumscribe space into place. Insinuating escape, death, and the record of lived experiences these matters are an attempt at understanding events that act as silent witnesses to history and only indirectly on the events themselves.

"The title derives from the musical term *mesure pour rien*, a silent measure at the beginning of a performance, a soundless interval conveying nothing but setting the tempo and so an essential part of the musical whole."[ii]

Braille Teeth originated from viewing a reproduction of an early drawing on typing paper by Jean-Michel Basquiat of a head including the
barely legible scrawl "BRAILLE TEETH," from 1980, and also appears
as one of the artist's graffiti phrases in the film *Downtown 81*. Known
for using subverted and absurd language-orientation in his work,
Basquiat exists as much as *Braille Teeth* similarly subsists in this text
as an emission for thoughts and ideas and as an individual seeking
to transcend boundaries, borders, and the trappings of place. *Nobody*
is directly taken from Jim Jarmusch's film *Dead Man*. A young man
in search of a new start, William Blake embarks on an exciting and
dangerous journey where a sense of an undiscovered West is found—a
West that vanished before it could be incorporated into national myth.
It is through this journey that *Nobody* guides William Blake through
the wilderness toward the northwest coast, in effect leading him
toward his own death. *Nobody*, who was once taken as a prisoner to
England and is well versed in the poetry of William Blake, is convinced
that this Blake is the poet himself. As an outcast, *Nobody* is of mixed
blood—he is half Blood and half Blackfoot; a strong and opinionated
Native American who was forcibly raised by whites and later given the
mocking name "Exaybachay, He Who Talks Loud, Say Nothing" by
fellow natives.

A note on the use of italicized text:

Sections that are italicized either set the scene or are used for stage
direction. In particularized areas of dialogue these segments also serve
as internal thoughts for each character, and set the mood for what
occurs, begins and ends.

TEXTS FOR NOTHING
Textes pour rien - after S.B.

Tragicomedy in two acts

"Then they set out along the blacktop in the gun-metal light, shuffling through the ash, each the other's world entire."[iii]

BRAILLE TEETH

NOBODY

ACT I

A road. A fence.

Evening.

They crossed through a fenceline or crossed where a fenceline once had been, the wires long down and rolled and carried off and the little naked mesquite posts wandering singlefile away into the night like an enfilade of bent and twisted pensioners.[iv]

BRAILLE TEETH. Hm! So here we are?[v]

NOBODY. Yes,[vi]

BRAILLE TEETH. And this is what it looks like?[vii]

NOBODY. Yes.[viii]

BRAILLE TEETH. ... Well, well, I dare say one gets used to it in time.[ix]

NOBODY. (*Stops, and peers downward.*) Look at this stuff. No growth, no decay, no streaming fluids.[x]

BRAILLE TEETH. ... a sort of perverse signature.[xi]

NOBODY. (*Turns and looks away.*) *To the east, he could see one of the concrete obelisks that stood for a boundary marker. In that desert waste it had the look of some monument to a lost expedition.*[xii] ... but I am very fond of such scenery. The distance in it is fluid and the contours vague, and thus perhaps it resembles my own position.[xiii]

BRAILLE TEETH. (*With an edge in his voice.*) Well, as far as I'm concerned, you won't get anywhere.[xiv]

NOBODY. But my attitude ... has not changed.[xv]

BRAILLE TEETH. Listen.[xvi]

NOBODY. I don't want to listen.[xvii]

BRAILLE TEETH. Don't the decapitated deserve recreation?[xviii]

NOBODY. I don't know. It's not working out.[xix]

BRAILLE TEETH. Everything here seems obscure and silent.[xx] (*With a delayed latency.*) ... an oppressive presence,[xixxi]

NOBODY. ... and ... nature's ... somewhat[xxiii]

BRAILLE TEETH. Concentrate, focus. Shape, color, texture, the parameters of beauty. Cultivate your garden. ... everything commences to grow and grow until[xxiii]

NOBODY. Ah, yes great mercies. What a blessing nothing grows, imagine if all this stuff were to start growing.[xxiv]

Pause.

BRAILLE TEETH. Imagine. For the moment.[xxv]

NOBODY. (*Gives BRAILLE TEETH a long stare, of feigned incredulity ... then his attention moves.*) I don't know. It's not working out. Maybe plants are too creepy, swaying between worlds, mind/no-mind, like what's going on there. It's scary. Now a rock is something that has weathered the crisis.[xxvi] Look at these specimens, for instance. Mass. Density. Permanence. Finality. Termination. The substance of walls, of fortification. Rock. Even the word conveys heft, a certain assurance. No loss of focus here.[xxvii]

BRAILLE TEETH. (*A little defensively.*) I've heard enough already. You've said enough. You've made the stones seem alive before my eyes.[xxviii]

NOBODY. Some halt in the way of things seems to work here.[xxix]

BRAILLE TEETH. Words, words, words.[xxx] You and your delirious quips![xxxi]

NOBODY. (*Begins to pace onward.*) *He walked up and back. His feet left cold wet tracks on the polished stones that sucked up and vanished like the tale of the world itself.*[xxxii]

BRAILLE TEETH. What are we looking for anyway?

NOBODY. What I am looking for is nowhere, as far as I can see.[xxxiii]

BRAILLE TEETH. You and your landscapes![xxxiv]

NOBODY. Strictly speaking I believe I've never been anywhere.[xxxv]

BRAILLE TEETH. Well the blood begins here....

NOBODY. ... and eyelids raise the curtain!

BRAILLE TEETH. What do you mean by that?[xxxvi]

NOBODY. What do I mean? (*Eyes* BRAILLE TEETH *suspiciously.*) I thought as much. That's why there's something so beastly, so damn bad-mannered, in the way you stare at me. They're paralyzed.[xxxvii]

BRAILLE TEETH. What are you talking about?[xxxviii]

NOBODY. Your eyelids. We move ours up and down. Blinking, we call it. It's like a small black shutter that clicks down and makes a break. Everything goes black; one's eyes are moistened. You can't imagine how restful, refreshing it is. ... little respites ... —just think! ...[xxxix]

BRAILLE TEETH. So that's the idea. I'm to live without eyelids.[xl] Tell me clearly, for conjectures have drawn me out of my home and muddled my thoughts.[xli]

NOBODY. Don't act the fool, you know what I mean. No eyelids, no sleep; it follows, doesn't it?[xlii]

BRAILLE TEETH. I shall never sleep again. But then—how shall I endure my own company?[xliii]

NOBODY. Try to understand. You see ... it's a second nature with me—.... Plaguing myself, if you prefer; I don't tease nicely. But I can't go on doing that without a break.[xliv]

BRAILLE TEETH. ... Ah, I see; it's life without a break.[xlv]

Short silence.

NOBODY. So's that's that.[xlvi]

BRAILLE TEETH. (*Shrugs his shoulders, mouth twitches.*) So one has to live with one's eyes open all the time?[xlvii]

NOBODY. To *live*, did you say?[xlviii]

BRAILLE TEETH. Don't let's quibble over words. With one's eyes open. Forever.[xlix] Why are you always so evasive?[l]

NOBODY. Remember you're not alone; you've no right to inflict the sight of your fear on me.[li] You keep us from seeing clearly.[lii]

BRAILLE TEETH. (*After prolonged reflection.*) One is what one is.[liii] I don't need your words in order to know who I am.[liv]

NOBODY. Well...

BRAILLE TEETH. Well what?

NOBODY. I never see you from where you see me.[lv]

BRAILLE TEETH. As if significance weren't burdensome enough.[lvi]

NOBODY. ... something is between us, I know it, I know it! Something is coming between us[lviii]

Silence.

BRAILLE TEETH. What did we do yesterday?[lviii]
NOBODY. What did we do yesterday?
BRAILLE TEETH. Yes.
NOBODY. Why ... (*Angrily.*) Nothing is certain when you're about.
BRAILLE TEETH. In my opinion we were here.
NOBODY. (*Looking round.*) You recognize the place?
BRAILLE TEETH. I didn't say that.
NOBODY. Well?
BRAILLE TEETH. That makes no difference.
NOBODY. All the same...
BRAILLE TEETH. (*Reflects. Then asks.*) In what direction did lost men veer?[lix]
NOBODY. (*Thinks.*) Perhaps it changed with hemispheres. Or handedness.[lx]
BRAILLE TEETH. What do we do now?[lxi]
NOBODY. In the meantime let us converse calmly, since we are incapable of keeping silent.
BRAILLE TEETH. You're right, we're inexhaustible.
NOBODY. It's so we won't think.
BRAILLE TEETH. We have that excuse.
NOBODY. It's so we won't hear.
BRAILLE TEETH. We have our reasons.
NOBODY. Have it your own way. I suppose we were bound to come to this.[lxiii]
BRAILLE TEETH. Such as?
NOBODY. All the dead voices[lxiii]
BRAILLE TEETH. They all speak at once.
NOBODY. Each one to itself.

Silence.

BRAILLE TEETH. Rather they whisper.
NOBODY. They rustle.
BRAILLE TEETH. They murmur.
NOBODY. They rustle.

Silence.

BRAILLE TEETH. What do they say?
NOBODY. They talk about their lives.
BRAILLE TEETH. To have lived is not enough for them.
NOBODY. They have to talk about it.
BRAILLE TEETH. To be dead is not enough for them.
NOBODY. It is not sufficient.

Silence.

BRAILLE TEETH. They make a noise like feathers.
NOBODY. Like leaves.
BRAILLE TEETH. Like ashes.
NOBODY. Like leaves.
BRAILLE TEETH. ... let me confess, you feel that way most of the time. You ache with the need to convince yourself that you do exist in the real world, that you're part of all the sound and anguish, and you strike out with your fists, you curse and you swear to make them recognize you. And, alas, it's seldom successful.[lxiv]

NOBODY. Well, I don't know that that's ... (*Trails off*) ... if that has anything to do with any ... thing.[lxv] Forget your sorrows ... Yesterday will never return.[lxvi] There were days when you peered into yourself ... and what you saw there made you faint with horror. And then, next day, you didn't know what to make of it, you couldn't interpret the horror you had glimpsed the day before.[lxvii]

BRAILLE TEETH. (*Admonishing.*) We've got to take what comes to us[lxviii]
NOBODY. If you can't trans-cend, you might as well descend.[lxix]

Long silence.

BRAILLE TEETH. Say something![lxix]
NOBODY. I'm trying.[lxxi]

Long silence.

BRAILLE TEETH. (*In anguish.*) Say anything at all![lxxii] My mind is troubled and can't keep silent.[lxxiii]
NOBODY. What do we do now?[lxxiv]
BRAILLE TEETH. Wait!
NOBODY. Ah!

Silence.

BRAILLE TEETH. This is awful!
NOBODY. Sing something.
BRAILLE TEETH. No no! (*He reflects.*) We could start all over again perhaps.
NOBODY. That should be easy.
BRAILLE TEETH. It's the start that's difficult.
NOBODY. You can start from anything.
BRAILLE TEETH. Yes, but you have to decide.
NOBODY. True.
BRAILLE TEETH. There's nothing for us here anymore. [lxxv]
NOBODY. (*... each ... stood apart from the other ... a sovereign form.*)[lxxvi] You here ... and I there.[lxxvii]

Silence.

NOBODY. Your silence clamors in my ears.[lxxviii]
BRAILLE TEETH. An inevitability.[lxxix]
NOBODY. (*After a long pause ... looking at him.*) Well, you can go on like that as long as you want to. And when you're done[lxxxx]

BRAILLE TEETH. (*Matter-of-factly.*) Is this our life?[lxxxi]
NOBODY. What you call our life feels like poison in my body.
BRAILLE TEETH. A pain I can't understand.
NOBODY. Stranger, my pain is the whole life I've lived.
BRAILLE TEETH. I'm wounded like you.
NOBODY. Ah yes, in your mind. But everything that goes on in one's head is so vague, isn't it?[lxxxii]

Silence.

BRAILLE TEETH. Help me![lxxxiii]
NOBODY. I'm trying.

Silence.

BRAILLE TEETH. When you ask you hear.
NOBODY. You do.
BRAILLE TEETH. That prevents you from finding.
NOBODY. It does.
BRAILLE TEETH. That prevents you from thinking.
NOBODY. You think all the same.
BRAILLE TEETH. No no, impossible.
NOBODY. That's the idea, let's contradict each other.
BRAILLE TEETH. Impossible.
NOBODY. You think so?
BRAILLE TEETH. We're in no danger of ever thinking any more.
NOBODY. Then what are we complaining about?
BRAILLE TEETH. Thinking is not the worst.
NOBODY. Perhaps not. But at least there's that.
BRAILLE TEETH. That what?
NOBODY. That's the idea, let's ask each other questions.
BRAILLE TEETH. What do you mean, at least there's that?
NOBODY. That much misery.
BRAILLE TEETH. True.
NOBODY. Well? If we gave thanks for our mercies?
BRAILLE TEETH. What is terrible is to *have* thought.
NOBODY. But did that ever happen to us?
BRAILLE TEETH. Somehow I feel we've never been so much alive as now. If we've absolutely got to mention this—this state of things, I suggest we[lxxxiv]

21

NOBODY. (*Fixing his eyes on him.*) Your mouth![lxxxv]

BRAILLE TEETH. (*As if waking from a dream.*) I beg your pardon.

NOBODY. (*With some irritation.*) Can't you keep your mouth still? You keep twisting it about all the time. It's grotesque.

BRAILLE TEETH. So sorry. I wasn't aware of it.

NOBODY. That's just what I reproach you with.

(*BRAILLE TEETH'S mouth twitches.*)

NOBODY. There you are! ... you don't even try to control your face.[lxxxvi] Your mouth looks quite diabolical that way.[lxxxvii] I won't let myself get bogged in your eyes. You're soft and slimy. Ugh! ... Like an ... Like a quagmire.[lxxxviii]

BRAILLE TEETH. (*Suddenly suspicious.*) Where are all these corpses from?[lxxxixw]

NOBODY. These skeletons.

BRAILLE TEETH. Tell me that.

NOBODY. You don't have to look.

BRAILLE TEETH. You can't help looking.

NOBODY. True.

BRAILLE TEETH. Try as one may.

NOBODY. I beg your pardon?

BRAILLE TEETH. Try as one may.

NOBODY. We should turn resolutely towards Nature.

BRAILLE TEETH. We've tried that.

NOBODY. True.

BRAILLE TEETH. Oh it's not the worst, I know.

NOBODY. What?

BRAILLE TEETH. To have thought.

NOBODY. Obviously.

BRAILLE TEETH. But we could have done without it.

NOBODY. Que voulez-vous?

BRAILLE TEETH. Ah! Que voulez-vous. Exactly.

Silence.

NOBODY. That wasn't such a bad canter.

BRAILLE TEETH. Yes, but now we'll have to find something else.

NOBODY. What now?[xc]

BRAILLE TEETH. Let me see.[lxxxi]

Pause.

NOBODY. (*Turning a little towards* BRAILLE TEETH.) Words fail, there are times when even they fail. Is that not so...? (*Pause. Turning a little further.*) Is that not so ... that even words fail, at times? (*Pause.*) What is one to do then, until they come again?[xcii]

BRAILLE TEETH. Let me see. (*Long silence.*) Ah![xciii]

NOBODY. Well?

BRAILLE TEETH. What was I saying, we could go from there.

NOBODY. What were you saying when?

BRAILLE TEETH. At the very beginning.

NOBODY. The very beginning of WHAT?

BRAILLE TEETH. This evening ... I was saying ... I was saying ...

NOBODY. I'm not a historian.

BRAILLE TEETH. Wait ... we embraced ... we were happy ... happy ... what do we do now that we're happy ... go on waiting ... waiting ... let me think ... it's coming ... go on waiting ... now that we're happy ... let me see ... ah!

BRAILLE TEETH. Let's just keep walking.

NOBODY. ... walking what's left of our wits.[xciv] Just remember that the things that you put into your head are there forever, ... You might want to think about that.[xcv]

BRAILLE TEETH. Yes. You forget what you want to remember and you remember what you want to forget.[xcvi]

NOBODY. In either case it's pretty close to nothing getting past.[xcvii]

BRAILLE TEETH. Look around you. Ever is a long time. The last instance of a thing takes the class with it.[xcviii]

NOBODY. (*He thought each memory recalled must do some violence to its origins. As in a party game. Say the word and pass it on. So be sparing. What you alter in the remembering has yet a reality, known or not.*[xcix] *After a pause. Then, as if remembering something.*) Out here, it's the tiniest stutter, the subtlest patch—an affordable loss of no significance.... Should a bit vanish from an event, we likewise manage.[c]

In the evening a wind came up and reddened the sky. They noticed the small dust that powdered their legs while walking across the dry bracken.

A sound without cognate and so without description.[ci]

BRAILLE TEETH. (*Deeply serious. His voice rising to match* NOBODY'S.)
But we are each that, while we live, however much we resist: almost without surface, barely contained,...[clicii]

NOBODY. (*In pensive thought.*) *What and how much had I lost by trying to do only what was expected of me instead of what I myself had wished to do?*[ciii]

BRAILLE TEETH. (*After a sympathetic pause. With a private knowledge.*) *He imagined the pain of the world to be like some formless parasitic being seeking out the warmth of human souls wherein to incubate and he thought he knew what made one liable to its visitations. What he had not known was that it was mindless and so had no way to know the limits of those souls and what he feared was that there might be no limits.*[civ]

Like some site of siege in an older time, in an older country, where the enemies were all from without.[cv]

Catastrophe lacked coherence. Every separate day was built anew and then dismantled at night, the successive constructions becoming less and less elaborate, lonely props thrown up against hope by a weariness so deep their bones felt tired with sand in their eyes.[cvi]

Dusk...

Night.

Curtain.

ACT II

Next day. Same time.

Same place.

They passed through ruins of an old ranch on that stony mesa where there were crippled fenceposts propped among the rocks that carried remnants of a wire... An ancient pickethouse. The wreckage of an old wooden windmill fallen among the rocks.[cvii]

A stone wall. A tower.

NOBODY. (*Watching the darkness until the spaces between the wall planks turned pewter, and then, even before the ... whistle, he went out into the cool gray ... evening, a white mist lifting over the field of weeds behind the ... tower, to look at the rubble in natural light. The changes were only subtle ones. The sand appeared ashen, the shattered lengths of jutting wood metallic. The wreckage was totally anonymous.*[cviii]) ... Perhaps you're shy of speaking first? Right. I'll lead off. (*A short silence.*) I'm not a very estimable person.[cix]

BRAILLE TEETH. (*Before he continued, he studied* NOBODY, *trying to gauge his response.*) Why, I wonder? If I search for the explanation it will not be impossible to find. Yet the important thing is whether or not you intend to listen to it. Anyway I realize that I'm putting on a one-man show, but I don't want to bore you.[cx]

NOBODY. One keeps putting off—putting up—for fear of putting up—too soon—and the day goes by—quite by—without one's having put up—at all.[cxi] If you are frank, if we bring our specters into the open, it may save us from disaster. So—out with it![cxii]

BRAILLE TEETH. (*Things will get worse*, he thought to himself. *Then better.*[cxiii]) ...well, quite frankly, I'd rather be alone. I want to think things out, you know; to set my life in order, and one does that better by oneself. But I'm sure we'll manage to pull along together somehow.[cxiv]

NOBODY. You think too much, that's your trouble.[cxv]

BRAILLE TEETH. One's got to think of something.[cxvi]

NOBODY. (*Considers it. Petulance creeping in.*) Let the shadows in to play their part![cxvii]

BRAILLE TEETH. (*Pauses ... not knowing quite what to do.*) What about it ... shall I go on, or ...?[cxviii]

NOBODY. —Yes, yes, if you make it short. [cxix]

BRAILLE TEETH. —Short? [cxx]

BRAILLE TEETH. (*With sudden vehemence.*) Seems like a concealment for a sensible evil.

NOBODY. What do you hope to get ...? Forgetfulness?[cxxi]

BRAILLE TEETH. (*Vaguely.*) ... in spite of myself.[cxxii] I came to the conclusion that I must resign myself to a choice[cxxiii]

NOBODY. (*After a moment's consideration. Thinks about it ... then.*) Within itself is concealed the premonition of it's end.[cxxiv]

BRAILLE TEETH. (*A mindful echo. Seriously, if sadly.*) *As they watched the slivers of light from the wreckage, he'd not have thought the value of the smallest thing predicated on a world to come. It surprised him. That the space which these things occupied was itself an expectation.*[cxxv] *All of this like some ancient anointing. So be it. Evoke the forms. Where you've nothing else construct ceremonies out of the air and breathe upon them.*[cxxvi]

Among the muted and scattered structures they waited...

NOBODY. (*Quietly, but with great intensity. As if from a distance.*) Damn, death is tiring.

BRAILLE TEETH. (*A hint of communion in this.*) Nothing for their struggles, nothing for their names. Nothing for the living or the dead.[cxxvii]

Long pause.

NOBODY. The laws are cruel on this point. The undone can't be patched or stretched. The wounds last.[cxxviii]

At the edge of the picket house stood a fountain. ... a trickle of dry brown fluid had slid down the stained beak and algae furred breast of a stone bird into a bowl of stagnant scum. The stone bird seemed to be getting fuzzier about the edges.[cxxix]

One thing at least is certain, in an hour it will be too late, in half-an-hour it will be night, and yet it's not, not certain, what is not certain, absolutely certain, that night prevents what day permits, for those who know how to go about it, who have the will to go about it, and the strength, the strength to try again.[cxxx]

BRAILLE TEETH. (*After a brief silence.*) —we know nothing.[cxxxi]
NOBODY. Nothing that counts.[cxxxii]
BRAILLE TEETH. We haven't yet begun to suffer.[cxxxiii]
NOBODY. I'm afraid you're mistaken.[cxxxiv] Everything in its place ... everything in its own good time.[cxxxv]
BRAILLE TEETH. (*Slowly, seeping with conviction.*) I'll never get any-where, but when did I? When I laboured, all day long and let me add, before I forget, part of the night, when I thought that with perseverance I'd get at me in the end? Well look at me, a little dust in a little nook, stirred faintly this way and that by breath straying from the lost without.[cxxxvi]

NOBODY. *He passed like an apparition through the banded rhomboid from the small window in the western wall. The routed dustmotes reeled.*[cxxxvii] Perhaps we are only too much in a hurry to burn ourselves out.[cxxxviii]

BRAILLE TEETH. (*Uncertainly.*) We were afraid of ... stopping before burning out, but we were not sure we wanted to go on the way people usually do.[cxxxix]

NOBODY. ... what a situation![cxl]

BRAILLE TEETH. We're—inseparables![cxli]

NOBODY. (*Reassuring. Looking about intently.*) Whatever lurks ahead of grievous abominations and disorder, you and me walk into it together.[cxlii]

BRAILLE TEETH. (*Very pointedly.*) Did I try everything, ferret in every hold, secretly, silently, patiently, listening? I'm in earnest, as so often, I'd like to be sure I left no stone unturned before reporting me missing and giving up. In every hold, I mean in all those places where there was a chance of my being, where once I used to lurk, waiting for the hour to come when I might venture forth, tried and trusty places, that's all I meant when I said in every hold. Once, I mean in the days when I still could move, and feel myself moving, painfully, barely, but unquestionably changing position on the whole, the trees were witness, the sands, the air of the heights, the cobblestones. This tone is promising, it is more like that of old, of the days and nights when in spite of all I was calm, treading back and forth the futile road, knowing it short and easy seen from Sirius, and deadly calm at the heart of my frenzies.[cxliii]

NOBODY. We only know something's the matter[cxlivv]

BRAILLE TEETH. Truth and illusion. Who knows the difference, eh...?[cxlv]

NOBODY. Truth and illusion ... you don't know the difference.[cxlvi]

BRAILLE TEETH. No, but we must carry on as though we did.[cxlvii]

NOBODY. Doesn't it matter to you ... at all?[cxlviii]

BRAILLE TEETH. (*Pause; then suddenly. Forcefully.*) My question, I had a question, ah yes did I try everything, I can see it still, but it's passing, lighter than air, like a cloud, in moonlight, before the skylight, before the moon, like the moon, before the skylight. No, in its own way, I know it well, the way of an evening shadow you follow with your eyes, thinking of something else, yes, that's it, the mind elsewhere, and the eyes too, if the truth were known, the eyes elsewhere too.[cxlix]

BRAILLE TEETH. (*With the beginnings of a knowledge he cannot face.*[cl]) But all things, ... all things, ... transmute..., life diminishes, everything, declines, the proliferation of kinds is a mere illusion, and no one knows to what end.[cli]

NOBODY. (*Discerningly.*) ... nothing prevents anything.[clii] ... No lists of things to be done. The day providential to itself. The hour. This is later. All things of grace and beauty such that one holds them to one's heart have a common provenance in pain. Their birth in grief and ashes.[cliii] (*Gesticulating. With finality.*) No lessons can be drawn from this however.[cliv]

BRAILLE TEETH. (*Ignoring the remark.*) You are laboring under a great delusion[clvclv]

NOBODY. (*With great, sad relief.*) ... waiting for the pain to subside and for hours doing nothing but looking out, early on induced me to imagine a silent catastrophe that occurs almost unperceived.[clvi]

BRAILLE TEETH. But now comes a colourless age.[clvii]

NOBODY. What in God's name are you talking about?

BRAILLE TEETH. (*As if he suddenly understood.*) Little is left to tell.[clviii]

NOBODY. Nothing is left to tell!

The entrance to nature's theatre stood open.[clix]

The grainy air. The taste of it never left your mouth. They stood in the rain like farm animals. Then they went on ... in the dull drizzle. Their feet were wet and cold. ... old crops dead and flattened. And the dreams so rich in color. How else would death call you? From daydreams on the road there was no waking.[clx]

In the nights in their thousands to dream the dreams of a child's imaginings, worlds rich or fearful such as might offer themselves but never the one to be.[clxi]

Sequences of retributive lightning cast across the zenith.

Panic dwindled into jitters into detached fascination. It was just a show. The longer they watched the less they felt. Events coupled, cavorted, and vanished, emotion hanging in midair before their lemur eyes like a thin shred of home- less ectoplasm. It was cool. It was like drowning in syrup.[clxii]

NOBODY. (*Quite beside himself.*) What I look back at with amaze- ment is the situations I accepted. I had undertaken, with my com- panion, to see it out, and I was under a charm, apparently, that could smooth away the extent and the far and difficult connections of such an effort.[clxiii]

BRAILLE TEETH. (*Calm. Then, determined, after a pause.*) Only the words "yesterday" and "tomorrow" still had any meaning for me.[clxiv]

NOBODY. *hmm* ... A blurred and generalized projection of you and me.[clxv]

BRAILLE TEETH. (*Solemnly. As if for the hundredth time.*) ... shadow and babble, ...[clxvii]

NOBODY. (*Expansively.*) ... a question unspoken, in the eyes of a mute, an idiot, who doesn't understand, never understood, who stares at himself in a glass, stares before him in the desert, sighing yes, sighing no, on and off.[clxvii]

BRAILLE TEETH. (*More or less to himself.*) He would like it to be my fault that he has no story, of course he has no story, that's no reason for trying to foist one on me. That's how he reasons, wide of the mark, but wide of what mark, answer us that.[clxviii]

Brief silence.

NOBODY. There has to be one, it seems, once there is speech, no need of a story, a story is not compulsory, just a life, that's the mistake I made, one of the mistakes, to have wanted a story for myself, whereas life alone is enough.

BRAILLE TEETH. (*Considers, then, immediately.*) ... I'll learn to keep my foul mouth shut before I'm done, if nothing foreseen crops up. But he who somehow comes and goes, unaided from place to place, even though nothing happens to him, true, what of him?

NOBODY. (*Poised, in a kind of limbo.*) I stay here, sitting, if I'm sitting, often I feel sitting, sometimes standing, it's one or the other, or lying down, there's another possibility, often I feel lying down, it's one of the three, or kneeling. What counts is to be in the world, the posture is immaterial, so long as one is on earth.

BRAILLE TEETH. (*Deeply serious.*) To breathe is all that is required, there is no obligation to ramble, or receive company, you may even believe yourself dead on condition you make no bones about it, what more liberal regimen could be imagined, I don't know, I don't imagine. No point under such circumstances in saying I am somewhere else, someone else, such as I am I have all I need to hand, for to do what, I don't know, all I have to do, there I am on my own again at last, what a relief that must be.

NOBODY. Yes, there are moments, like this moment, when I seem almost restored to the feasible. Then it goes, all goes, and I'm far again,

with a far story to begin, to end, and again this voice cannot be mine. That's where I'd go, if I could go, that's who I'd be, if I could be.
BRAILLE TEETH. (*Makes a hesitant move forward, avoiding* NOBODY.)

A long silence presented itself as clouds convened and evening weighed down on their crowns.

BRAILLE TEETH. (*Strangely, with distinction.*) Always so deliberate, hardly surprised by the most outlandish advents. A creation perfectly evolved to meet its own end.[clxix]

Pause.

BRAILLE TEETH. So here we are,[clxxx]
NOBODY. (*As if the word were unfamiliar to him. Waiting out the interruption, not really paying it any mind.*) Hm? (*Realizing.*) Oh, I'm sorry. I wasn't even listening … or thinking … (*With a flicking of his hand.*) … whichever one applies.[clxxxi]

After a sympathetic pause.

BRAILLE TEETH. (*Remembering. Then aloud, but to* NOBODY'S *retreating form.*) … but what is this evening made of, this evening now that never ends, in whose shadows I'm alone, that's where I am, where I was then, where I've always been, it's from them I spoke to myself, spoke to him, where has he vanished, the one I saw then, is he still in the street, it's probable, it's possible, with no voice speaking to him, I don't speak to him anymore, I don't speak to me anymore, I have no one left to speak to, and I speak, a voice speaks that can be none but mine, since there is none but me.[clxxii]

Silence. Outwardly calm.

NOBODY. (*... softly, slowly ... almost whispering. ... As if from a distance. With dignified finality ... to the point where there is something to lose.*[clxxiii])Is it possible, is that the possible thing at last, the extinction of this black nothing and its impossible shades, the end of the farce making and the silencing of silence, it wonders, that voice which is silence, or it's me, there's no telling, it's all the same dream, the same silence, it and me ... but whose, whose dream, whose silence, old questions, last questions, ours who are dream and silence, but it's ended, we're ended who never were, soon there will be nothing where there was never anything, last images.[clxxiv]

A long silence between them.

Curtain.

ENDNOTES

ACT I

i.   Ackerley, Gontarski, *The Grove Companion To Samuel Beckett: A Reader's Guide to His Works, Life, and Thought.* Texts for Nothing. p. 563.
ii.   Ibid., p. 563.
iii.   McCarthy. *The Road.* Knopf, 2006. p. 5.
iv.   Cormac, McCarthy, *The Crossing.* Volume Two: *The Border Trilogy.* Vintage International, 1994. p. 73. (italics added).
v.   Jean-Paul Sartre, *No Exit And Three Other Plays.* Vintage International, 1989. p. 3.
vi.   Ibid., p. 3.
vii.   Ibid., p. 3.
viii.   Ibid., p. 3.
ix.   Ibid., p. 3.
x.   Stephen, Wright, *Meditations in Green.* Vintage International, 1983. p. 264
xi.   Wright, *Meditations in Green.* p. 279.
xii.   McCarthy, *The Crossing.* Volume Two: *The Border Trilogy.* p. 74. (italics added).
xiii.   Kobo, Abe, *The Box Man.* Vintage International, 1973. p. 42.
xiv.   Jean-Paul Sartre, *No Exit And Three Other Plays.* Vintage International, 1989. p. 8.
xv.   Cormac McCarthy, *All the Pretty Horses.* Volume One: *The Border Trilogy.* Knopf, 1992. p. 136.
xvi.   Shadi Abdel Salam, *The Night of Counting the Years, Al-Mummia.* Film. 1969.
xvii.   Ibid.,
xviii. David Milch, *Deadwood.* TV Series. "Season Two, Episode Eight". HBO, 2005. DVD.
xix.   Wright, *Meditations in Green.* p. 264.
xx.   Shadi Abdel Salam, *The Night of Counting the Years, Al-Mummia.* Film. 1969.
xxi.   Stephen Wright, *Meditations in Green.* Vintage International, 1983. p. 91.
xxii.   Ibid., p. 91.
xxiii. Stephen Wright, *Meditations in Green.* Vintage International, 1983. p. 90.
xxiv.   Paul Auster, *Samuel Beckett: Dramatic Works. The Grove Centenary Edition.* Volume III. "Happy Days". Grove Press, 2006. p. 289.
xxv.   Ibid., p. 5.

xxvi.   Wright, *Meditations in Green*. p. 264.

xxvii.   Wright, *Meditations in Green*. p. 264.

xxviii.   Shadi Abdel Salam, *The Night of Counting the Years, Al-Mummia*. Film. 1969.

xxix.   Cormac, McCarthy, *Child of God*. Vintage International, 1973. p. 156.

xxx.   Wright, *Meditations in Green*. p. 264.

xxxi.   TV On The Radio, "Snakes and Martyrs" from *Return To Cookie Mountain*. Interscope Records, 2006.

xxxii.   Cormac, McCarthy, *All the Pretty Horses*. Volume One: *The Border Trilogy*. Knopf, 1992. p. 206.

xxxiii.   Ackerley, Gontarski, *The Grove Companion To Samuel Beckett: A Reader's Guide to His Works, Life, and Thought*. Introduction. Anywhere and Nowhere: Mapping the Beckett Country. p. ix.

xxxiv.   Samuel Beckett, *Waiting for Godot*. Act II. Grove Press, 1954. p. 40. (edited).

xxxv.   Ackerley, Gontarski, *The Grove Companion To Samuel Beckett: A Reader's Guide to His Works, Life, and Thought*. Introduction. Anywhere and Nowhere: Mapping the Beckett Country. p. ix.

xxxvi.   Jean-Paul Sartre, *No Exit And Three Other Plays*. Vintage International, 1989. p. 5.

xxxvii.   Ibid., p. 5.

xxxviii.   Ibid., p. 5.

xxxix.   Ibid., p. 5.

xl.   Jean-Paul Sartre, *No Exit And Three Other Plays*. Vintage International, 1989. p. 6.

xli.   Shadi Abdel Salam, *The Night of Counting the Years, Al-Mummia*. Film. 1969.

xlii.   Jean-Paul Sartre, *No Exit and Three Other Plays*. Vintage International, 1989. p. 6.

xliii.   Ibid., p. 6.

xliv.   Ibid., p. 6.

xlv.   Jean-Paul Sartre, *No Exit And Three Other Plays*. Vintage International, 1989. p. 5.

xlvi.   Jean-Paul Sartre, *No Exit And Three Other Plays*. Vintage International, 1989. p. 22.

xlvii.   Jean-Paul Sartre, *No Exit And Three Other Plays*. Vintage International, 1989. p. 6.

xlviii.   Ibid., p. 6.

xlix.   Ibid., p. 6.

l.   Shadi Abdel Salam, *The Night of Counting the Years, Al-Mummia*. Film. 1969.

li.   Jean-Paul Sartre, *No Exit And Three Other Plays*. Vintage International, 1989. p. 9.

lii.   Shadi Abdel Salam, *The Night of Counting the Years, Al-Mummia*. Film. 1969.

liii.   Samuel Becket, *Waiting for Godot*. Act I. Grove Press, 1954. p. 14.

liv.   Shadi Abdel Salam, *The Night of Counting the Years, Al-Mummia*. Film. 1969.

lv.   Jacques Lacan, *Book XI: The Four Fundamental Concepts of Psychoanalysis*. "Of The Gaze As Objet Petit a". *The Line and Light*. W. W. Norton & Company, 1981. p. 103.

lvi.   Kay, Ryan, *The Niagara River. Poems*. Grove Press, 2005. p. 16.

lvii.   Carl Jr. Laemmle, James Whale, Frankenstein: The man who made a monster. DVD. Universal Pictures Production. 1931.

lviii.   This and the following nine quotes are all from Samuel Beckett, Waiting for Godot. Act I. Grove Press, 1954. p. 10.

lix.   McCarthy, The Road. p. 98.

lx.   Ibid., p. 98.

lxi.   This and the following six lines of quotes are all from Samuel Beckett, *Waiting for Godot*. Act II. Grove Press, 1954. p. 40–42. (italics added).

lxii.   Jean-Paul Sartre, *No Exit And Three Other Plays*. Vintage International, 1989. p. 23.

lxiii.   This and the following nineteen lines of quotes are all from Samuel Beckett, *Waiting for Godot*. Act II. Grove Press, 1954. p. 40–42. (italics added).

lxiv.   Ralph Ellison, *The Invisible Man*. Vintage International, 1947. p. 4.

lxv.   Edward Albee, *Who's Afraid of Virginia Woolf?* New American Library, 2006. p. 179.

lxvi.   Shadi Abdel Salam, *The Night of Counting the Years, Al-Mummia*. Film. 1969.

lxvii.   Jean-Paul Sartre, *No Exit And Three Other Plays*. Vintage International, 1989. p.42.

lxviii.   Jean-Paul Sartre, *No Exit And Three Other Plays*. Vintage International, 1989. p. 10.

lxix.   Stephen Wright, *Meditations in Green*. Vintage International, 1983. p. 264.

lxx.   Samuel Beckett, *Waiting for Godot*. Act II. Grove Press, 1954. p. 41.

lxxi.   Ibid., p. 41.

lxxii.   Ibid., p. 41.

lxxiii.   Shadi Abdel Salam, *The Night of Counting the Years, Al-Mummia*. Film. 1969.

lxxiv.   This and the following eleven lines of quotes are all from Samuel Beckett, *Waiting for Godot*. Act II. Grove Press, 1954. p. 41.

lxxv.   Shadi, Abdel Salam, *The Night of Counting the Years, Al-Mummia*. Film, 1969.

lxxvi.   Stephen Wright, *Meditations in Green*. Vintage International, 1983. p. 293.

lxxvii.   Jean-Paul Sartre, *No Exit And Three Other Plays*. Vintage International, 1989. p. 17.

lxxviii.   Jean-Paul Sartre, *No Exit And Three Other Plays*. Vintage International, 1989. p. 22.

lxxix.   Edward Albee, *Who's Afraid of Virginia Woolf?* New American Library, 2006. p. 125.

lxxx.   Edward Albee, *Who's Afraid of Virginia Woolf?* New American Library, 2006. p. 173.

lxxxi.   This and the following four lines of quotes are all from Shadi Abdel, Salam, *The Night of Counting the Years, Al-Mummia*. Film. 1969.

lxxxii.   Jean-Paul Sartre, *No Exit And Three Other Plays*. Vintage International, 1989. p. 19.

lxxxiii.   This and the following twenty-four lines of quotes are all from Samuel Beckett, *Waiting for Godot*. Act II. Grove Press, 1954. p. 41.

lxxxiv.   Jean-Paul Sartre, *No Exit And Three Other Plays*. Vintage International, 1989. p. 12.

lxxxv.   This and the following four lines of quotes are all from Jean-Paul Sartre, *No Exit And Three Other Plays*. Vintage International, 1989. p. 12.

lxxxvi.   Ibid., p. 9.

lxxxvii.   Jean-Paul Sartre, *No Exit And Three Other Plays*. Vintage International, 1989. p. 20.

lxxxviii.   Jean-Paul Sartre, *No Exit And Three Other Plays*. Vintage International, 1989. p. 41.

lxxxix.   This and the following twenty-one lines of quotes are all from Samuel Beckett, *Waiting for Godot*. Act II. Grove Press, 1954. p. 41. (italics added).

xc.   Paul Auster, *Samuel Beckett: Dramatic Works. The Grove Centenary Edition*. Volume III. "Happy Days". Grove Press, 2006. p. 284.

xci.   Samuel Beckett, *Waiting for Godot*. Act II. Grove Press, 1954. p. 42.

xcii.   Paul Auster, *Samuel Beckett: Dramatic Works. The Grove Centenary Edition*. Volume III. "Happy Days". Grove Press, 2006. p. 284.

xciii.   This and the following eight lines of quotes are all from Samuel Beckett, *Waiting for Godot*. Act II. Grove Press, 1954. p. 42.

xciv.   Edward Albee, *Who's Afraid of Virginia Woolf?* New American Library, 2006. p. 35.

xcv.   McCarthy, *The Road*. p. 10.

xcvi.   Ibid., p. 10.

xcvii.   Ryan, *The Niagara River. Poems*. Grove Press, 2005. p. 53.

xcviii.   McCarthy, *The Road*. p. 24.

xcix.   McCarthy, *The Road*. p. 111.

c.   Ryan, *The Niagara River. Poems*. Grove Press, 2005. p. 70–71.

ci.   McCarthy, *The Road*. p. 220. (italics added).

cii. Ryan, *The Niagara River. Poems.* Grove Press, 2005. p. 36–37.
ciii. Ralph Ellison, *The Invisible Man.* Vintage International, 1947. p. 266. (italics added).
civ. Cormac McCarthy, *All the Pretty Horses.* Volume One: *The Border Trilogy.* Knopf, 1992. p. 256–257.
cv. Cormac McCarthy, *All the Pretty Horses.* Volume One: *The Border Trilogy.* Knopf, 1992. p. 208–209. (italics added).
cvi. Stephen Wright, *Meditations in Green.* Vintage International, 1983. p. 272. (italics added).

ACT II

cvii.   Cormac McCarthy, *All the Pretty Horses*. Volume One: *The Border Trilogy*. Knopf, 1992. p. 23. (italics added).
cviii.   Stephen Wright, *Meditations in Green*. p. 202. (italics added).
cix.   Jean-Paul Sartre, *No Exit And Three Other Plays*. Vintage International, 1989. p. 24.
cx.   Abe, *The Box Man*. Vintage International, 1973. p. 168.
cxi.   Paul Auster, *Samuel Beckett: Dramatic Works. The Grove Centenary Edition*. Volume III. "Happy Days". Grove Press, 2006. p. 289–290.
cxii.   Jean-Paul Sartre, *No Exit And Three Other Plays*. Vintage International, 1989. p. 23.
cxiii.   Arundhati Roy, *The God of Small Things*. Random House, 2008. p. 274.
cxiv.   Jean-Paul Sartre, *No Exit And Three Other Plays*. Vintage International, 1989. p. 9.
cxv.   Jean-Paul Sartre, *No Exit And Three Other Plays*. Vintage International, 1989. p. 39.
cxvi.   Jean-Paul Sartre, *No Exit And Three Other Plays*. Vintage International, 1989. p. 38.
cxvii.   Burnt Sugar: The Arkestra Chamber, "Castles Made of Sand" from *The Sirens Return/Keep It Real Till It Flatlines*. Trugoid, 2001.
cxviii.   Abe, *The Box Man*. Vintage International, 1973. p. 168.
cxix.   Ibid., p. 168.
cxx.   Ibid., p. 168.
cxxi.   Jean-Paul Sartre, *No Exit And Three Other Plays*. Vintage International, 1989. p. 45.
cxxii.   Ralph Ellison, *The Invisible Man*. Vintage International, 1947. p. 19.
cxxiii.   Simone de Beauvoir, *She Came to Stay*. W. W. Norton & Company, Inc. p. 15.
cxxiv.   Abe, *The Box Man*, Vintage International, 1973. p. 168.
cxxv.   McCarthy, *The Road*. p. 159. (italics added).
cxxvi.   McCarthy, *The Road*. p. 63. (italics added).
cxxvii.   McCarthy, *The Road*. p. 301.
cxxviii. Ryan, *The Niagara River. Poems*. Grove Press, 2005. p. 54.
cxxix.   Wright, *Meditations in Green*. p. 222–224. (italics added).
cxxx.   Paul Auster, *Samuel Beckett: The Grove Centenary Edition*. Volume IV. *Poems, Short Fiction, Criticism*. "Texts For Nothing". Grove Press, 2006. p. 297. (italics added).
cxxxi.   Jean-Paul Sartre, *No Exit And Three Other Plays*. Vintage International, 1989. p. 23.
cxxxii.   Ibid., p. 23.

cxxxiii. Jean-Paul Sartre, *No Exit And Three Other Plays*. Vintage International, 1989. p. 10.

cxxxiv. Edward Albee, *Who's Afraid of Virginia Woolf?* New American Library, 2006. p. 209.

cxxxv. Edward Albee, *Who's Afraid of Virginia Woolf?* New American Library, 2006. p. 64.

cxxxvi. Paul Auster, *Samuel Beckett: The Grove Centenary Edition*. Volume IV. *Poems, Short Fiction, Criticism*. "Texts For Nothing". p. 314.

cxxxvii. Cormac McCarthy, *The Crossing*. Volume Two: *The Border Trilogy*. Vintage International, 1994. p. 42. (italics added).

cxxxviii. Abe, *The Box Man*. Vintage International, 1973. p. 173.

cxxxix. Ibid., p. 173.

cxl. Jean-Paul Sartre, *No Exit And Three Other Plays*. Vintage International, 1989. p. 42.

cxli. Ibid., p. 42.

cxlii. David Milch, *Deadwood*. TV Series. "Season Two, Episode Two". HBO, 2005. DVD.

cxliii. Auster, *Samuel Beckett: The Grove Centenary Edition*. Volume IV. *Poems, Short Fiction, Criticism*. "Texts For Nothing". p. 316.

cxliv. Ryan, *The Niagara River. Poems*. Grove Press, 2005. p. 3.

cxlv. Edward Albee, *Who's Afraid of Virginia Woolf?* New American Library, 2006. p. 213.

cxlvi. Edward Albee, *Who's Afraid of Virginia Woolf?* New American Library, 2006. p. 214.

cxlvii. Ibid., p. 24.

cxlviii. Edward Albee, *Who's Afraid of Virginia Woolf?* New American Library, 2006. p. 217.

cxlix. Auster, *Samuel Beckett: The Grove Centenary Edition*. Volume IV. *Poems, Short Fiction, Criticism*. "Texts For Nothing". p. 316.

cl. Edward Albee, *Who's Afraid of Virginia Woolf?* New American Library, 2006. p. 249.

cli. W.G., Sebald, *After Nature*. Random House, 2002. p. 51.

clii. Auster, *Samuel Beckett: The Grove Centenary Edition*. Volume IV. *Poems, Short Fiction, Criticism*. "Texts For Nothing". p. 339.

cliii. McCarthy, *The Road*. p. 46. (italics added).

cliv. Ryan, *The Niagara River. Poems*. Grove Press, 2005. p. 24.

clv. Franz, Kafka, *The Trial*. Shocken Books, 1937. p. 11.

clvi. Sebald, *After Nature*. Random House, 2002. p. 89.

clvii. Sebald, *After Nature*. Random House, 2002. p. 95.

clviii. Samuel Beckett, *Ohio Impromptu, Catastrophe, and What Where:* Three Plays by Samuel Beckett. "Ohio Impromptu". Grove Press, 1984. p. 15.

clix. Sebald, *After Nature*. Random House, 2002. p. 101. (italics added).

clx. McCarthy, *The Road*. p. 16-19. (italics added).

clxi. McCarthy, *The Road*. p. 23. (italics added).

clxii. Wright, *Meditations in Green*. p. 18. (italics added).

clxiii. Henry, James, *The Turn of The Screw, and Other Short Novels*. Signet Classics, 1995. p. 308.

clxiv. Albert, Camus, *The Stranger*, Vintage International, 1988. p. 80.

clxv. Ryan, *The Niagara River. Poems*. Grove Press, 2005. p. 52. (italics added).

clxvi. Auster, *Samuel Beckett: The Grove Centenary Edition*. Volume IV. *Poems, Short Fiction, Criticism*. "Texts For Nothing". p. 334.

clxvii. Auster, *Samuel Beckett: The Grove Centenary Edition*. Volume IV. *Poems, Short Fiction, Criticism*. "Texts For Nothing". p. 324.

clxviii. This and the following five quotes are all from Paul Auster, *Samuel Beckett: The Grove Centenary Edition*. Volume IV. *Poems, Short Fiction, Criticism*. "Texts For Nothing". p. 307.

clxix.   McCarthy, *The Road.* p. 50.
clxx.   Jean-Paul Sartre, *No Exit And Three Other Plays.* Vintage International, 1989. p. 46.
clxxi.   Edward Albee, *Who's Afraid of Virginia Woolf?* New American Library, 2006. p. 49.
clxxii.   Auster, *Samuel Beckett: The Grove Centenary Edition.* Volume IV. *Poems, Short Fiction, Criticism.* "Texts For Nothing". p. 333.
clxxiii. Edward Albee, *Who's Afraid of Virginia Woolf?* New American Library, 2006. p. 131.
clxxiv.   Auster, *Samuel Beckett: The Grove Centenary Edition.* Volume IV. *Poems, Short Fiction, Criticism.* "Texts For Nothing". p. 338–339.

I am indebted to Steffani Jemison for reaching out to me then and now. I am honored to participate in her vision. Without her guidance and insightful criticism my contribution would not exist.

I am deeply grateful to Tricia Van Eck for taking a risk in me and for the continued support over the years. Thank you for the many significant suggestions and for the long conversations. Your keen observations and thoughts helped shape this publication.

A grateful acknowledgment goes to Sebastian Civarolo for making this an exquisite compendium.

Texts for Nothing
Copyright © 2011 *Harold Mendez*

ISBN: 978-0-9833815-4-9

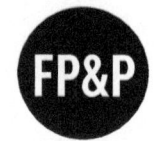

future plan and program

Future Plan and Program
http://futureplanandprogram.com

Please direct inquiries to:
thefuture@futureplanandprogram.com

Series editor: Steffani Jemison
Series designer: Sebastian Civarolo

Future Plan and Program was incubated in 2010-2011 by Project Row Houses.

Acknowledgements: Danielle Burns, Justin Cavin, Aisen Chacin, Ashley Clemmer-Hoffman, Cheryl Flores, Quincy Flowers, Hannah Ireland, Philip Jemison, Steven Jemison, Rick Lowe, Jasmine Jamillah Mahmoud, Phyllis McCallum, Solkem N'Gangbet, Michael Peranteau, Nikki Pressley, Linda Shearer, Martine Syms, Michael Kahlil Taylor, and Julie Thomson.

Future Plan and Program was generously funded in part by the following individuals: Kerry Inman & Denby Auble, John Roberson & John Blackmon, Danielle Antoinette Burns, Justin Cavin, Jereann Chaney, Melody Clark, Ashley Clemmer Hoffman & Brendan Hoffman, Phyllis L. McCallum and Steven Jemison, Joey Romano & Nicole Laurent, Victoria Thomas McGhee, Scott Sawyer & Michael Peranteau, Gregory & Diane Schultz, Leigh & Reggie Smith, and Rebecca Trahan. Special thanks to Jill Whitten & Robert Proctor.

Funding for Steffani Jemison's residency at Project Row Houses was provided by: The National Endowment for the Arts, the City of Houston through the Houston Arts Alliance, Houston Endowment Inc., The Brown Foundation, The Kresge Foundation, The Andy Warhol Foundation for the Visual Arts, and the Texas Commission on the Arts. Steffani Jemison's residency was part of a collaboration with the Core Program at the Glassell School of Art of the Museum of Fine Arts Houston.

www.ingramcontent.com/pod-product-compliance
Lightning Source LLC
Chambersburg PA
CBHW030744200526
45160CB00007B/4